EARS

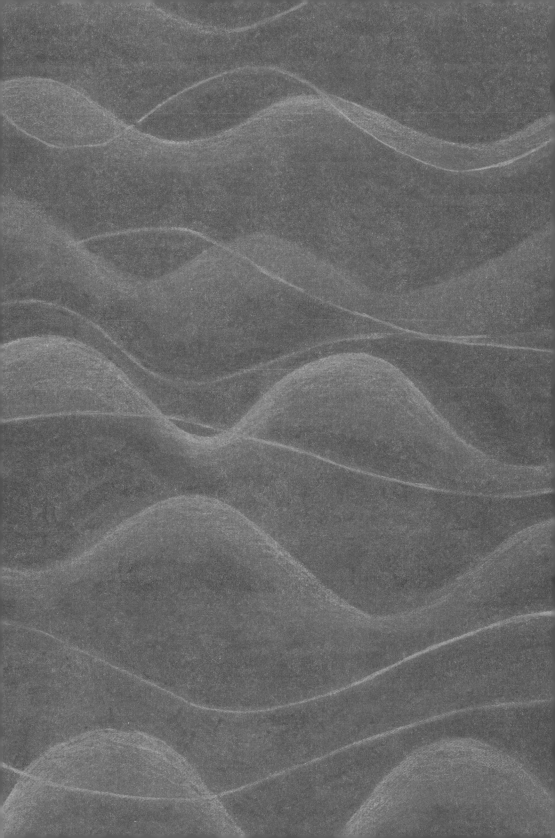

EARS

Jared Stanley

NIGHTBOAT BOOKS

NEW YORK

ISBN: 978-1-937658-62-5

Design and typesetting by Mary Austin Speaker
Text set in Granjon

Cover Image: Julia Schwadron, Ears, 2016

Cataloging-in-publication data is available from the Library of Congress

Distributed by University Press of New England
One Court Street
Lebanon, NH 03766
www.upne.com

Nightboat Books
New York
www.nightboat.org

MIX
Paper from
responsible sources
FSC
www.fsc.org   FSC® C011935

Contents

Reverberation

Often I am caught watching the sun

tick off the days it takes the earth

to go around it. In the change of angles

at which anything enters my window

and these rooms, our heavy

conjoined breath produces a superior,

malodorous glee at waking; well, we

do avoid kissing, first thing. There's

a heavy skein of dewlets arranged

in a polygon, a coldness at morning.

Well, the furnace broke down. The

frosted shingles on each rooftop help

the houses imitate the peaks

of the Carson Range, themselves dusted.

And I'm looking; I'm looking and

wishing to talk, and an irrational thing

pulls me from the chair, goddammit.

Some fog comes, and then

the next thing you know

I'm shaded in a canyon creek.

Where are you? I'm talking to the sun,

then to all the barefoot things in the canyon

and, leaning on a scarp, the cuffs of my pajamas

are getting pretty damp in the shady humus.

I'm not in the house: in the shadows

of the Range's canyons.

To avoid inscribing or memorializing

anything that passed between me and

the bugs, the leaves, the ancient,

slow motion geology, and the rare water

each of these presences implies,

I shall overlay the events with the following,

culled from my collection of pseudoscientific

works: ANOTHER CURIOUS

PIECE OF THE JIGSAW APPEARED

IN *THE ELECTRICAL EXPERIMENTER*,

JUNE 1920, IN WHICH DR. J.B. RANSOM,

CHIEF PHYSICIAN OF THE CLINTON PRISON,

REPORTED ON THIRTY-FOUR CONVICTS

SUFFERING FROM BOTULINUS POISONING.

ONE TRIED TO THROW AWAY A PIECE

OF PAPER AND FOUND IT STUCK TO HIS HAND;

SOON ALL THE AFFLICTED WERE IN THE SAME

HIGHLY CHARGED CONDITION, VARYING

IN INTENSITY WITH THE SEVERITY OF THE

POISONING. With such an interlude or mask

I keep the canyon to me like the secret it was

and this anecdote acts as a strikethrough,

a textbook of hiding. There really was (you'll have to trust me)

a solar interaction between this House-in-the-

Shape-and-Guise-of-a-Mountain, and I, its

Queen-Under-the-Hill-and-Timekeeper.

I was taken away and brought back

and despite myself an invention came in:

a single, unified speech, un-original,

utterly humid with all sorts of microbial situations

and though I'd love to tell you about it, my

poetry wants quite badly to be part of the real world

so I put that stuff about magnetic bodies in here

the real world on top of my memory

my hovering, and my desire.

= * =

Lenticulars, like broad-beamed anime space cruisers

take up all the sky over the Virginia Range, to the

(you'll have to trust me) southeast of the guise.

Mica winks from the ground surrounding Blue Mass

in the Schell Creek Range. These place names

are particular to a marginal state often enough

at the bottom of a list of all fifty,

the kind of desert that exposes its rough edges

when driven through or flown over: sparse,

as many mountain ranges as Afghanistan.

The places it's made of don't need my voice-over

and my relative hiding or exposure might

take on fifty different meanings when ultimately

it all comes to coyotes or vultures,

any type of scavenging friend that might

come around and give my waning

flesh a little shelter. I'll give no cutaway

here, no substitute for vile wonderment,

no antiseptic range of conjured images

from one time or another, no gibberish

treading the history of science

with a succession of trivial spoofs.

But it is basically trivia. I invoke these old

places, their young names and the ochre

slash marks made in a cliff's cavity

by ancient artists with old fingers.

They're here now and it makes no difference.

You'll never go there or see it, which could be

one kind of difference. There are plenty of places

a bit too close to California's border

for a proper refuge, so you go there:

you keep Tahoe blue

you have a Steller Jay scream in your ear;

if the poem was made of reason and change

I could strike a careless pose.

It's not. I won't.

October

When I prop the left

side of my head up on my

left hand, my heart starts

beating in my right ear;

the hairs on that ear catch

the last of this year's sun

heat, so there're spectral

filigrees in the hairs which

cover that lobe in

tiny prisms (these days

have emphatic color)

prismatic like the leg

hairs of pre-pubescent

boys and girls—I

was one of those

once, staring at

my shins; the hairs

exactly the same as

the hairs on Katrina's,

who was on the floor

with her legs straight out

her back propped up

on a plush mauve ottoman

at the after school bible study

group somebody or other

convinced me to go to.

Katrina was Christian.

Staring at her legs

and at mine was

how I endured it,

an embedded-

in-my-person person,

an animist even, and

interested in whether

she was embedded in hers

and whether hairs in general

were, as Danny in

Withnail & I said,

"your aerials."

The children of

the family who

hosted the bible

study were spoiled.

Animism explains

why I stole action

figures from the back

of their untidy closet,

an act of malice set

against the chintzy

iconoclasm in

the living room,

a presentation or

warning to my

forebears' prohibitions

against dancing, their

love of yelling —

anyway what

is more animist

than a Transformer?

October is

a turn in the poem

neither the end

of a romance

nor the start

of a tragedy,

one more golden

age out in the

future beyond the

thin-skinned touch

of public discourse

upon my soft tissue

which needs a whole

tube of ointment

squirted upon it.

No.

October is full

of Libras, born under

the gentlest sign

time of harvest

of steadily cooling

abundance, in which

we say goodbye

to the absurd

threats that wizards

of finance make:

they think they

extinguish us

with surveys,

we who, in the guise

of the teacher and the

saunterer, predate

them, and prey

upon their fear

which spreads

like a cliché

for we are

in point of fact

their elders

in our avocation

or enthusiasm

and we drink their

spitting ignorance

for sustenance

or aver or talk over

or mock them in

our native tongue,

wherever in

the amnesia that

came from

to live in and on,

like worms or the

hairs of Katrina,

or a boat,

or a lake,

itself anew.

It's Art my friend,

my friend—

in the golden age

my heart it beats

with both my ears

with nothing to

remember so

there's nothing

to forget,

combed finely along

these comely ears, such

a pause in them, such

a pink, lop-eared

yeti or chimera

in the golden age

or its purple years

or its white fur

and my heart

skips to beat

it out in all

such ears

Slept on it Wrong,

so I can't keep my mind cold

       enough to hover from mountain

     to mountain to mountain

on a lightness of color,

     in my empyrean

hair glitter - I wanted to

     mean anything,

anything frail, even—

       and could be

could not be without my body

 in that pain, its

dimensions numerous as muscles:

       a thought. And if

I had a thought

  there'd be stars (under my eyelids)

 if I tried to move my arm

      for consolation

    in motion

  I could think it

and only see stars

when I moved my arm

there was a pop, up in my sleep

at the top

of my spine, center

of my mind: I mean, I was *screaming!*

I have loved this body too much

in its humorous juxtapositions to be

screaming at it

like a thing

I was born to be all up in.

*

So the world's in

the way it makes you squint.

Wince rhymes with quince.

I saw one once, in Oxfordshire…

brought to mind in

the richness which returns to life

after bodily pain has stopped.

If poetry were the way to do it,

I'd wish such abundance on our

friends whose pains do not subside

how they still hover in their bodies

from mountain to mountain to mountain

can still consider the fundament,

how one takes the air, how one

enjoys the chicken and waffles,

can still take such delicate care

with their heads inclining flowerward

in the forthrightness of bodily pain,

typing and shaping and figuring out problems.

Seamless in touch. In conversation

rarely crying out. They are strong people.

Herm

We walked openly and for no reason

To form in the prowl of talk an owl's head insignia—

That's one way to say we took a walk

Or that rabbit brush dusted our sleeves

With pyramidal hints

With imitative and contagious music

Which gave these nights, in their broad coolness

A gift to come into, a

Bee sting on an Adam's apple.

We loped to propose a question:

If the poem is an axis, what

Are the lines which cross it,

Its immersions, its alongsideness?

And I take upon me this speaking for both of us,

Confined as we are to the poem, its

Crossed figurations, its eye-encircled

Constellating, crossed and re-crossed by the paths and piths

of spy novels, of hot wings,

Of little cuts of grease in the cuticles,

Of my coat, leaking feathers,

Of any decorative response.

I push one fingernail under the other

And feel some pressure on my foot:

Either the sock is too big or the shoe is too small

Knowledge outpacing the desire to know

Our walk's aim, a creeping deliverance,

A fresh set of tracks at angles, willy-nilly,

Parti-eyed to within an inch of home.

These genial squiggles turn inside the wit

Which animates such a walk

Its etymologies and hidden laws heaped up

In the thousandfold litter, the lichens

And tiny pebbles in a cairn; will they allow us

To well up in this unfurling,

This flag, this Russian roulette we're playing

With a crystal ball?

The words at war seem to shrink

From memory forth to possession;

Look out at the war. We are at the path

At the stump, at the ford, at the rise,

Where we were ever at rest in this poem…

And spiders crawl from my clothes.

Wan joy, they scatter toward the mutable shade;

The neighborhood's outskirts are full of hawks

And there's always this music playing.

Is this re-telling of the walk

An accompaniment? Either I am

Accompanying your sitting down with a tale

Of nouns achieved on a walk,

or you are the destination of this poem

In which "interest disguises hope"

And spandrels full of powerful feathers

And the phlegmatic faces of

The seraphim fill the roof of heaven.

They seem so calm in their energetic heat,

Circling the throne and chanting.

Does that fire-making motion radiate out and down?

Well, the hot skin on my neck says *yes*,

And that such a walk is an emulation,

An accompaniment, aspirant to

The form of the finch's flight

Full of loping dignity,

A dream of great personal fastidiousness

That shadows my trust as I fall toward you

Having stumbled over a large rock;

The shadow of my trust falls about you

Very ably laughing together a single form.

And so, there is this kind of relentlessness:

The owl talk, the commerce with the dead,

With the resolutely inhuman,

The creatures and stones, and our dead friend,

That sum of a boy who shadowed us

As we skirted the city, considering

His ears, and ours, made for details,

That he must still hear the music and hawks in his death

Hear the yogurt falling like snot onto my zipper.

And whose white hair is this

Caught between my nose and the bridge of my glasses?

Like it, you see me, the poem made by _____,

Only by shadow, umbra solis, or by moon,

So as to quiet what a reader prompts

In the words that form.

Let morning be morning

A shape at rest;

The stars reflected in

A shovel aren't dim

They don't exist.

Tune for Drum and Wind

You're a wandering blare

a weird sounding hunger

called fire, living it

another in a series of public breaths

flutter my pantleg like coyote teeth.

I'm not sure: should we be decorous

and let the wind beat

a drum beyond our life

and ability to do so?

It *could* be alright on its own

if we leave the drum out

in all the click-clack weather

the fronds and licks of fluent heat

and wind's vivid skin-ingratiations

talking directly into the tympanun.

We could just throw the drum

at the weather, accompany it

with the air we stashed in the snares

so it touches our liberty

our radiant, quintessential vase

made from book light and

unscrewed from practical terms.

Fragments of the space shuttle Columbia fell here

full of toiletries, your money, and a false grail called survival.

After that, somebody else came,

new to us, blurting a tattered note

in rhythms we use to disappear, one into the other.

[One Reason to Gain Years]

One reason to gain years

and become venerable and majestic

is that you can go all

various, horizontal

and omnidirectional

with your geomantic peculiarities,

so I went to Nevada

almost at will, almost

an adept of years

a colt or filly cantering

Hyundai-wise by a roadcut

the very picture of geologic scale.

I'm pretty sure I'm a sorcerer,

so I'm getting a lot of job offers here

BUT the only thing I quiver to do

are some hollow imitations

of my own indivisibility

by treating a list of visible trees

as an obstacle course, a test of skill,

mimicry, imitation, and group

psychosis: I keep your shape, apple;

your leaves get covetous of high country blue, catalpa;

you're a poor ornamental, Siberian elm;

help me become the lower atmosphere's furrier, cottonwood.

It's either these tests of skill or sleep

beneath a fir with cones

which disintegrate at maturity

to release winged seeds.

The kids walk by.

Otter Pops in blue

in orange.

It's touching and various

out on the lawn, these years like this

like something a dog would do

an open trick, composed of ears

that hang in and scratch out

the asymmetrical eyes of air;

if you're hearing with one

swinging lance of pure capture

more toward the reader's interest

than the small flies

that glint the world full

of all my catching, all my wing

all my droplets and this fruit

then it's August,

complete as the stranger

I encrust with my heart.

And, just so you know I am

who I say I am

a starling gurgles

and enters the conversation,

small insects flit from burr to burr

a scrap of rag's thrown over

a shard of star thistle.

That's how it is, to scatter out

toward the mandate of inanimate friendship.

From The Sea Ranch

          My skin changes direction, migrates

to sleep. 'Sleep' means 'I tongue at my left eye

as it slowly descends into its socket

          from heaven as if by a chain

'til my tongue won't reach.'

Little honeybee sucking at the cup-shaped eternity:

The left eye has its unbuilt plan,

as if a city: Ecbatan

      Xanadu

          Cibola

             Winnemucca

          The looming of outskirts in starlight.

And *by* starlight, I touch cities projected

onto the eye's convex arrangement. I pry open

the lid a sliver; the roof gives way

to a cold and open dome, its sister sphere:

both blink in the pinpricks of their names (eye and sky)

I lip their sibling sounds, moan a bit and toss, pull the sheet

Between my legs in Shangri-la.

In smooth pursuit of our rest

sleep has no singular attention:

but hey hey hey

neither of us

Has a song to guide

the other either

so who's to say or

suss or chant?

Lulla, lulla

shafts of noctilucent gray

smack the brim of a leaking hat

this means mentally reconstituting paradise

But hey - now what?

Don't blink me to sleep.

Don't blink mean sleep?

Don't its blinking mean sleep?

Somehow we open

the heavy front door

and both fit through

while holding hands

awake-seeming, barefoot

but sleeping.

Four porcelain cups wait for us outside

in the mossy gravel.

It feels like a ritual

gray light, damp.

Eight eyelids almost touch

many lashes shield the slits.

They're porcelain coffee cups like my grandma's,

decorated with North American songbirds

brims lined in real gold

the kind that spark in the microwave.

The cups like nothing else

the pelican, the hedge

muted but visible.

Blink go the lights on the opposite side of the bay,

the eyelid's memorial to waking.

We pluck out our eyes

place one in each cup

cup each with both hands

kneel as if putting an egg on the ground;

it seems the thing to do.

The eyes slide on a film of tears

into the brim neatly

the cups like new skulls

as if the blood in our heads had been granted the right

to give off that rich dull color of gold seen by candlelight

though I don't know what you're thinking

while you yank on yours

plucked whole from some sockets,

our eyes stick like jelly to the lip of the cup

and when spilt, like slugs to the soil.

Others are asleep in the next room.

Can they hear our breath

its dignified beat, almost a footfall

in this folie à deux

when you and sleep escape me?

In Pierces

On G Street

under the plucked pomegranates

to make a dry sound is best

if there are no men around

to walk like death to work

on the balls of their feet

on the tips of their lonesome werewolf feelings

on the "can't feel" of their endemic faces.

Not pierced or impressed by tongues,

I'm a watching creature

my habitat the entropic demand

of lesser jewels,

agate/turquoise/zirconia,

the decorative

tail of a Chinese Spaniel

hachiya-orange in bare trees,

a raccoon's corpse changed

to coyote's muscle, to ant's blood.

So utterly pierced by the aching

slowness of quest, of years—

a single tongue rinses the inside of my mouth

with callligrammic gamelan bells.

I eat drunk waxwings whole:

their plain decorous effusion,

the bells, the knells,

the hollow green yells,

they carom off the heart like fat.

The year came alive and wet

so a dry soul is best

under the plucked pomegranates

of G Street.

Abundance

I like to think the world is dead and

Pretty when fireworks hit the trees:

My eyebrow hairs spark; I entertain

The notion. Sound & vision &

Burnt hair smell: the world as dead.

Don't get me wrong; it's more

Than a tinge to write after its fact

Way off in the distance like a truck with fumes.

Beige scrubland with Funyon wrappers.

A life among these friends, why is it

So cute for it to look so dead?

I wanna destroy all the old shapes

That prey on my mind

And the new ones that'll appear

After my eyeballs swarm with the legs

Of ants feeding on only matter:

I have a copper deposit in my eye.

Just to think of the legs scuffing

Across my eyeball gives all eight

Senses an excuse for urgent

Inhuman hope: even a

Disappointed creature's eyes will

Someday finally turn to stone.

That's the grunting, *that's*

The texture of feeling required

If you want to feel like you're a part

Of any last generation, one that feels this way

Or that about the great and abiding

Terror of day. But what the hell does

That mean? Day is day. Terror is theater.

Day is slow and attracted to

The beyondtime after the ants

And bacteria (a beyondtime measured

Out with one body only - absurd

But lyrical) toward which one

Habitué of afternoon

Is called, like waves or by the moon

In a furling twitch of distraction.

The garbage truck's brakes squeak.

A voiceover, I tend to believe

Stupid things and will them into being crucial

By chanting them, once or many times:

Sophia dropped a veil over the divine realm,

And speech is its filigreed pattern.

I'm called to believe that because it

Sounds good, because it

Helps me understand why I love it

When Werner Herzog says "Squirrel"

Why it's comforting to have proof

Of others who share my name:

The atheist in Oklahoma City

The art professor at Bob Jones University.

I'm glad they seem to have a shape

At least as interesting as a dream life

Or the youth I can barely recall

In whose days we used to admire

People who refused to be brought low

Into the busywork and tidying-up of a single day.

But now, brought to a point where my ass

Looks alien in the hotel mirror,

There's an equanimity I find

At odds with the words I loved (and love)

To toss around, words like "crisis," words

That cut from the teeth in a way

That doesn't quite fit a competing

Sense of calm charm that flowers

Out from a noontime in June or

Weeks earlier in the cockeyed new

Weathers in which I touch a permission

I find with my fingers, the light

In an evergreen shrub, a niche

Between abstract power, its metadata,

And a close, direct, touching kindness.

Who knows, a single source for it

Like death to us but carrying on

Past our fantasies of destruction.

Who wants to live in a fantasy

Of proof, or the texture of any

Forest's canopy? Aflame or calm,

Those refuges among the weird trees

And confusing whistling reveal measures,

Emotions that balance and then are

Declarations of an imbalance:

The English beards of Hawaiian kings

Old prose descriptions of the sound of

Eucalyptus leaves scratching each other

In a hot wind. I get confused in my trust

At times, often in daylight: Are those

The screams of invasive birds or children?

Is the form of a marsupial an argument?

I wish there was a name for it when

Everyone forgets their own dependence.

A huge truck revs fumes all up in

My face on purpose, shaking up the

Unshakeable world. What the day's doing

In its gaily obfuscating blossom

I don't know, so I watch myself hurl,

Casually anyway, toward

Another small calamity

In my industry, climb around

In my husk and push out toward

A variety, a genteel sense

Of time, then molt to become an interstice

In some others' time, close as

A wiggle in the brain, nearly music

But precisely time, a power of

Intimacy drawn into the chest

Through the ears where wit has long in-

Truded, supplanting conversation

But opening out toward its semblance,

In which talking is basically the definition

Of skin and the word *love* is thrown

Around too easily. But it's true:

The common jackrabbit has a place

In my heart, a shallow depression

In the earth where it births its kits. It's—

That this is their world and any sense

I have of it is pretty dim,

A forgotten dependence, lacking in

Detailed smells and intuitive greetings

—A day, the next. The eye only goes

So far, and here you can see far, hear far,

But why confuse it, why tangle it

In the gossamer effusions of

The poem, earthchild, or any trick o'

The mind, when our task is to be

Unsurprised by a future which comes

On with an easiness and certainty

Shot through with zealous foibles: someone

Whispers *bacon* over the intercom.

Let me put it this way: are we to be

As astrologers, and predict the behavior

Of some unseen and semi-permanent power,

To find a fundamental way to

Greet the days as they come, to find a

Confidence somewhat like a steady

Undulating cloud? The dog absentmindedly

Licks my ankle. My eye starts to twitch

Like unsolicited advice, leading it

To quiver among its parts

As unsurprised as possible by

The end of our world as they knew it.

To find a cadence out there, even in

The effluent which passed through the blood

Barrier in my friend's brother's brain

After he gulped some sewer water

Surfing off San Diego. Who

Could've seen it? Some poems are

Only instructions, still points, dimes,

Muddy droplets: how to live, what to do.

"Think like a jackrabbit, let them think

You're extinct; Change the habitat, we

Creatures call it hiding;" or "we'll all

Have tender feet in the new world." Do

These console? At first they're sensitive

Then the feet grow calloused, hard.

Equanimity is a kind of

Retreat, an adaptation. But isn't

Poetry as much the fertile

Making of a new sense of how we

Might hide in a copse of unfamiliar

Invaders as it is a resistant

Place for imagining new ways of

Crying out alongside phenomena

Like dreamy bioengineering

Which is bullshit until it saves your life?

They promise to make me smarter but

The whole thing's so strenuous.

I wanna be dependent.

My equanimity folds together

In a barely known cadence

And to barely know it is

A trick I learned from desert creatures

Crawling on their bellies

Or hopping from thorn to thorn.

And if I barely hold it in my ear

How do I speak of a future

When there's so much to be clasped and

Reheld together by the convivial

Self-organization of observation?

Anyway my childhood marshes

Will be gone when I'm old, inundated

By the ocean like I'm inundated

By the day. Memorials? No.

…I might be forgetting my own dependence

Trying to haunt the world I was born into,

Full career variety of tidbits,

Lit from below, put the TV in front

Of the picture window. Clouds shrouded

In clouds, other touches…who you are

To me, and I to you as you read

This? Did you become an interstice?

An idea I have about you.

In the slick light off these fronds,

I'm as jealous of the heavy colors

As I am of the droplets which hit

The tip of each leaf like a drum.

I move often toward dream, which has its

Own fundamental untranslatability,

A property it shares with the future

And the word *apple*. If I described

The birdsong you'd think I was lying

But then there's no explaining who's

Fooling who in the animal arts

Of deception, instruction

And equanimity, ancient as

The shape of a blink, but

Younger, by far, than the day.

That's Cassiopeia

At the heart like the silver rivet

That holds the parts of the planisphere together

My Friend, My Amulet

We get an ageless thing to occur

a sweet and lunar gravity

in reading, the star of pleasures

flicker to demonstrate that dignity

is light kept in a necklace for touch

and won't refuse to answer to memory

safe and apart from skin. Costume glass

is worn air rayed about the person

like a sousaphone, a tone

noontime light surrounds my rights,

oblivious to the clavicle and its scoop

of gravity, gathering place of facets.

Legs

At the tip of the start of another

creature's life, I don't barely

belong to the ground I love:

the forest of youth rhymes

eucalyptus and vibraphonist,

empty of all letters but

resplendent, either because

another creature's coming

to us or because a distant

part of this body's past,

the loose confederation of

symbolism, floppy hats, and

strings of beads hanging from

the low branches of the cypress trees

in the Polo Fields are instances

of muscle memory, brought into

the present by bobbing my head

righteously to unheard music,

a stately peace that seems

to inhabit these knock-off

Tiffany lamps, pix

of Bob Kaufman, weirdly-lit

donut shops' plastic chairs,

rampant enumeration, any kind of shirt

with one-button buttoned, a big beige

toenail poking out of a buffalo sandal…

all of it clots up the belonging

of a day. Foremost among the

attachments which emerge from afternoon

fogs, the stateliness and antique

weirdo-hood of that ground I love

is *Legs*, by Barbara Shawcroft,

a weirdly inert yet intricate pile

of DuPont-made textile three stories tall,

affixed by a large metal brace to a wall

at the east end of the Embarcadero BART Station.

Apparently a giant pair of legs.

It looks like it's never been cleaned,

a creature made of discarded

rigging tossed over generations

of ships in Yerba Buena Cove.

I used to stare, pleased that someone'd

put such a bulbous, dusty mass in this place,

rising from the bowels of the station

a little Geryon, a plug in the drain.

The station keeps its hulking, brutalist calm.

Untrained but impressed enough

to lose my sense to this herm

I turned from the path and knotted up

the way, made up some stark bullshit

to guide this body through its intermingled

trials and comedic frisson

the way one goes along, as if there was

any such thing as a thing that went.

Just hanging there, ill-lit and neglected,

Legs suggested other body parts,

that if one had the stomach and luck

each of which sound like ideas but

may just as well be glands, phalanges

or walk-through hearts

(at least in a world like that City)

where fortitude and luck were at least

as present as fog, regular self-reinventions,

of senses in a world on the edge of a world.

Well if one had the stomach and luck

one could translate the vastness

of its secrets, folds, and and knots,

its sheer incongruity, its leaking

whispers or dusty cascades

of synthetic, tightly-wound fiber

its fundamental muteness

describing a certain fondness or deference

to out-and-out material,

rather like Yngwie J. Malmsteen,

rather like K.K. Downing,

and Sylvia Juncosa

and Buck Dharma lived by,

the stately, ungrounded

buzz of the thing on the thing

you plunked your thumb against, and *there*…

growing old in its station, growing thicker

more unfamiliar as the years' soot came

to encrust it, a sea giant, a great organism,

mutely, as it comes, bringing all of the station

into its netherworldly calm.

There's an article on the KQED website

that covers the proposed removal of *Legs*

from the station. One commenter says:

I always found that thing to be kinda gross and creepy.

Why on earth would anyone put something that would

attract so much filth into that environment?

Its filth is a thicket, a lump

on the edge of the forest of youth

a stately clump, a knotted

lovespace hanging from a wall

you could crawl in or cling to:

Legs gets its power

from its age not its novelty

its connection to an old idea

of the City that decided *Legs*

was a good idea, a City that

grew away in the world of my love

gray in the noon non-sun

away from coy fabulism

and the ear hair of agéd

shopkeepers.

Do I hate it?

I have attacks of

possessive enthusiasm

and love its imaginary softness

mystic but calm, replete with

San Francsico's Burning

San Francisco's Gone

Jan Yanehiro's pageboy and turtlenecks

that Polk Street occult bookstore

the word bathhouse as it was used on TV

the basement of Grant St. Records

full of Factory Benelux LPs

weird amatuerish euro-pop

obscure atonal disco —

the other days after the

other days in the City

formerly Venusian

with all these fears

to hope all up in.

I lose heart in it all the time

but always come back around

to the archaic throatedness it engenders

an off-color faith in these

old-fashioned instruments

tuned for an early music:

in manuscript, a tune I barely hum,

though the performance goes somewhere entirely

out of the ability of any head to contain—

I get a little bit loose and hotly fear the place

its wine, love and observation

how it made me a child

a native of homelands

of Greece, of Chang-An,

of Tenochtitlan;

and *Legs*.

Poem

keep on keepin' on

truckin'

goin' with the flow

doin' what I can

keepin' my head on straight

pluggin' away

keepin' my head down

pullin' on my walkin' shoes

doin' what I can

goin' with the keepin' on

truckin' my head on straight

doin' what I'm pullin'

pullin' my head down

keepin' with the flow

pullin' what I can

doin' what I pull

pluggin' what I keep

Public Poem in Three Parts

In the steam room, at the gym

where my belly drains out over

the towel at my waist, sitting

with other gentlemen, slightly

bent forward, our hands on our thighs

our arms slightly bent, water

dripping from the ceiling; the

whole place smelling, as my nose

gathers it, of eucalyptus oils.

*

To tell it light, at the speed of touch:

our sensible bodies raveled and unravelled stillly,

in feral, high altitude sunlight, in domestic shades

too, and, more conventionally, alongside fingernail

clippings and emails from Albuquerque,

the voice tone of the radio correspondent's

bland equivocations only jargon. Like birdsong.

Is this activity some kind of rich, dull afternoon of life,

groped at in the shadow of the Herman Miller

Aeron Chair, some respite, that M&M ground

into a square of plastic carpet?

*

Pythoness, I need to make touch happen with you.

The Listening

Since what's around

them is called weather

and is full of sounds,

even determined

people are subject

to the listening

they can't exclude:

A tiny scavenger

bird squawks and

an ear just can't

hide the suggestion

the hairs try to

pick out in its cry,

since the trials

of friendship

between the squawk,

the ear, the hair,

and the head are

good, untimely.

Your hands cup their

love against any

extremity.

All kinds of winds

lick and suck on

the ears as they

practice the unseen,

sticking out toward

the outer limit

of what "being

determined"

could mean, to

ignore or insist

or overlay

a method of life

or authentic mist

over some totally

admixed eardrum buzz

and secret drone hum.

You could try to

stopper your mind

go deaf at concerts

hollow the resonant

disk of the head

to within a

hair's breadth

of a notion,

but then you'd be

measuring a silent

aversion against

the very thing

determination

is meant to destroy:

ears are an organ of fate.

For you and me though,

(whatever shape

we may be) it's

only physical

to say how we

could try and forget

that we ever tried

to detach a fond

or aggressive

quality from

the swift gerunds

in a day's

weathering

(the only kind

we jab and jab

our ears out into)

determined to

confuse tragedy

with comedy

both in the ears'

weird inflorescing

and in their studious

mishearings:

insects in circles

surely must be making

a strong, cumulative gust

about the head, taking

the shape of an

ampersand or

the shape of a dick,

though no sense organ's

mistakings could

return the earth to

the acoustic shape

it presented right

before the first

memory hollowed

out the second sound,

as when a prophetic

heat exhausts itself

with a star metaphor,

a thing a thing

does to itself

but which leaves all

the ears of history

in the light of a star

they cannot bear to hear—

oh well, that frees us up

to run either of

our heads over

the Cleopatra

coffee mug

the hard rice stuck

to last night's placemat

the white paint fused

to the flathead

screwdriver's handle

that little cut

on the Asian pear

over there, the roll

of plumber's tape

the postcard from

Korea folded

in half, a sack

of Mandarins

an illustration

of shark morphology

in a book left

open on the table:

I saw the figure 5

over the Ampullae

of Lorenzini,

the sharks' organ

for perceiving

electricity

and slight muscle

movement, for

orienting

a shark to the

magnetic field

of the earth. The

illustrated

ampullae can't

sense my fingers

slight twitch, though their

animate counterparts

have been sensing

pulses from the hearts

of their prey for

sixty-five million

years, so they don't

need an outer ear

or you to whisper

the word *extinction*

in high pitches in

their ocean and they

don't even need a brain

to know—it pulses

about them, up close,

under their snouts.

It's happened before,

their death, my death,

and yours, but

not even that

focusing chill

can return the earth

to our existences

spread across its

surface. Fine.

The eye, the ear,

the moment, none.

Fine. I never had

ampullae anyway

so I can't feel

anything, barely

oriented to

the magnetic field

of the earth, so

nobody knows where

in time I'm talking

from and at, least

of all nobody,

that unfeeling slough,

determined to

unfeel me. Snob.

I'm sure I'm dead,

that the idea of

November has been

adjusted to reflect

new realities,

sagebrush habitat

climbing the Eastern

flank of the mountains,

naturally. Burn them

to desert, to the

sound of a world.

Desert's weathers

won't support much life

that isn't low to

the ground, and their main

forms of communication

with themselves are

revenant whistles

over greasewood and

shadscale. Sagebrush

is a kind of wormwood.

Relax. This specific

emptiness (the

desert's) is not

about you, it's

about nobody,

but not about you

specifically

though it doesn't

mind if you use

it as a place to

store your feckless

ears, curse its

attention to your

tiniest sounds;

grit in your teeth

squeaks in time

to your jaw.

Nobody else

can hear it, but

you've swallowed

grit and made some

noise with your mouth.

Endeavor to feel

the pattern as heart,

a most fond interest

which, in this enchanted

beige, the desert greens

itself to be, green

as the face of

absinthe, green as

roadside cheatgrass in this

creepy weather.

Soon, these fields will

burn themselves

innocent as fire.

Relax. Endeavor.

Determine to love

the implacable

and unnoticeable,

ignore what the deserts

whisper to each other

when I say I love you:

when you hang towels

and bras from doorknobs,

(themselves refractive,

cheap crystals) the straps

and corners make

a music of clicks

when the window

is thrown open

onto a full-loving,

arid wind, your

intimates of

a fabric with

the signs and wonders

the desert has

on offer. So

enchantment has to

include, I guess,

the familiar goodbye

of winds come and gone:

it's their practice of

renunciation

I've come both to hate

and believe in when

I give a finger

or ten back to the

winds that made them

weathervanes in the

first place, the special

repatriation

at the tip of

my fingers'

touching core.

Like a burial,

a touch at air is

just another

practice of

abundance and

variety, the

opposite of hate

and hating my body.

Abundance itself

must be some force

of determined

enchantment minus

a list of words

like enchantment,

a listened-in void

roughing up the ears

which prefer to

hear what they wanted

to hear. What a strange

responsibility

for a sense organ

to bear, that you might

lop if off to spite

the overheard.

The reasonable,

appliance-like

hum at the center

of the poem

clicks on and off

all night, the hollow

at the center

of air forced

throughout the house

a revenant

of a revenant

a brown noise

alongside the

actions of any

cute and sleeping mind—

I'm clinging too hard

to being awake,

a damn fool

overhearing

my listening

but that's an

ancient feeling,

like skin and day

an arbitrary

measure, earshot

sure, or echolocation

anything to get

out from under

the eye and its light:

sun, the surveilling

enemy of the

moon in the sky

(called the moon)

moon only there in

the height of the

sun's lax oversight:

so this listening

is determined

dusk-work,

invisible

crepuscular

measure, maybe

a better way

to steal back

the ear's touch, its

sensitive love,

from the full sun

bright but only part

a half-measure

mistaken for

an obvious example:

"Stand out of my light!"

But since our ears

are only passers-by

on this old world which

aerates the brain

as it twirls around

on its spiny top,

the head a perch

for occasional wisps,

we hope and sense

we must be of a piece

with our dumb statements

and mercenary

friends, people

who say things like

"all society's

problems started

with the Walkman"

—even if you're

that kind of mirror-

hearer and demi-

moron and you

put your ideas

on your head like

a helmet of

determination,

you're still of a piece

with the unshielded.

Sorry.

It makes a detailed

wrinkle on my head

but I like solace

so I trust that

air's still meddlesome

and, still or unsettled,

it strikes your face

and *that* strikes my fancy,

though it's not going

to do much besides

make me feel better

about looking like an

old fool or young fool

(depending on the

level of attention

to time): just so,

my attempt to focus

on stealing my

overhearing back,

on peeling the

canal's layers of

wax back fail, fail.

It's a drag. The

poem wasn't

supposed to be

polemic, it was

supposed to be

about ears finding

their independence

from the will—

Fail. Fail. Glare. Hear.

These are letters,

official, tiny

parabolic

microphones:

what sense!

Blow your nose and

the shape of your

belly changes; each

organ on or in

our bodies wants

to gather pulses,

measures, sounds

blood, food, or baby's

lives, so I eat

this hamburger,

put on this winter

weight and say the

only thing that's not

the end: "It's not

the only end" I said,

"and anyway,

what's an end

when 'listened to'

and 'listening'

are both a funeral

and a christening?"

Mountain Mahogany

Noctilucent clouds

Purple light on the hills at night—

Something halfwit grand about

mistaking the air over mourning

doves' wings for the teakettle,

warm in here, inside the war

of ears—which one will point

a touch out toward the clearly

relevant silence no sound

can pull the air outside of

when wind makes my house a flute?

It's odd to call it a deed, but

the combed over rabbitbrush

and yellowy pollen which

covers my knee all changeably

interfingers me: with wind-shape,

as with anything strewn across

the mouth and part of its skillset,

what you reach out with matters,

the poor descendant tongue licks

various animalcules as it calls

up the well-balanced semblances

that hollow the scraggy looming

of mountain mahogany, thorny

on the ridgetops, big gaps between

much that is ear-rendered and calm

and much else that is neither

but then touch is much clearer

on the subject of wind than

wind is, though wind is passing

clear on the subject of dust

Pauses

Palpable somnia is a book's work.

There's a wasp's nest in this statue's armpit.

Warm rabbit urine on my ring finger.

These Sub-Vangelis-Muzak-Psychological-Warfare-Test-Subject kinds of feelings.

Being a weirdo is expensive.

The pruning of these lemon trees, the morass of these figs.

Furiousity.

An infinity of shoes.

Body spray.

"The age-old ruses of fishes and insects."

Vodka, milk, and Cup o' Noodles.

"to build up a world of strange books / in the absence of faith"

Shells and trees: cue Slayer.

Dude at the front of the pharmacy line scratches his beard with a credit card.

Do libertarians wash their hands?

Possible dust clouds next eleven miles.

Think and the mouth's a pore.

Hot dogs and white wine.

"It rained in Mecca despite being 109 degrees."

A pleasure escapes the eye.

"It could've been anyone's iconoclasm that did them in—it could've been mine."

Sarcastic dreams.

Polymer foliage.

"It was either insecticide or horse tranquilizer."

What's the best way to remember the War's inside us?

Unnovative.

If the wind's right, doves look like falcons.

Powder free latex exam gloves.

Her dad looked like a giant hippie oak tree.

"Gypsum Cave Served as an Ice Age Latrine for Giant Ground Sloths For
    Thousands of Years."

Death of a Musician

Some people have old names

but don't live very long

Hammond organ, battered Tom:

and he was one of those primitive fretboards

whose spare and peripheral movements

curled sorrow, fear and joy into one

outer ear, tuned up high like an E.

Could you be like that, someone else

among the promise of unheard music

spare and peripheral, too much self

to be someone late one afternoon,

obstinate, shimmering, recondite?

Slingerland, Nachos, Guild Starfire,

Grill Cheese sandwich. Music goes another way.

Dirty pint glass. Sour Gummy Bear,

unexplored harmonies culled

from mistakes in rehearsal. The blue

and errant drywall composed around them,

something pentatonic stuck in the dirty

carpet, some felicity and surprise

for a few years and then, monstrous

as Anubis, as chest hair, as California

in silhouette tattooed on your tit

a music came in. Listen Jack.

Acknowledgements

Versions of these poems originally appeared in *Bombsite (Bomb Magazine), Clade Song, Dreamboat, Manor House Quarterly, The Occupy Wall Street Anthology, Omniverse, No Infinite, pallaksch.pallaksch, Pangyrus, Peaches & Bats, textsound.org, Where Eagles Dare*, and in pamphlets from *Double Burst* (with Ted Rees), and the *Envelope Pamphlet Series*. Abiding gratitude to the editors of these publications.

Thank you to Stephen Motika and Lindsey Boldt and Mary Austin Speaker and Julia Schwadron.

This book is a product of conversations with David Abel, Megan Berner, Greg Burge, Allison Cobb, John Coletti, Peter Culley, Christina Davis, Sandra Doller, William L. Fox, C.S. Giscombe, Richard Greenfield, Matthew Hebert, Laura Henrikson, Emily Hobson, Nathan Hoks, Lauren Levin, Sandra Lim, Chris Martin, Catherine Meng, Laura Moriarty, Meredith Oda, Felicia Perez, Ted Rees, June Sylvester Saraceno, Steve Seidenberg, Cedar Sigo, Patricia Smith, Gabie Strong, Brian Teare, Catherine Theis, Alli Warren, Laura Wetherington, Stephanie Young, and the Reno Ramblers.

For Eleanor.

JARED STANLEY was born in Arizona, grew up in California, and now lives in Nevada. He is the author of three books of poetry: *Ears*, *The Weeds*, and *Book Made of Forest*. Stanley has received fellowships from the Nevada Arts Council and the Center for Art + Environment and teaches writing and interdisciplinary art at Sierra Nevada College.

NIGHTBOAT BOOKS

Nightboat Books, a nonprofit organization, seeks to develop audiences for writers whose work resists convention and transcends boundaries. We publish books rich with poignancy, intelligence, and risk. Please visit our website, www.nightboat.org, to learn about our titles and how you can support our future publications.

The following individuals have supported the publication of this book. We thank them for their generosity and commitment to the mission of Nightboat Books:

Elizabeth Motika

Benjamin Taylor

In addition, this book has been made possible, in part, by grants from The National Endowment for the Arts and The New York State Council on the Arts Literature Program.